Pro
Musica
Antiqua

ProMusica Antiqua

Poems by
O. B. HARDISON, JR.

LOUISIANA STATE UNIVERSITY PRESS

Baton Rouge and London 1977

Designer: Dwight Agner
Type face: VIP Baskerville
Typesetter: Graphic World, Inc., St. Louis, Missouri

A number of these poems have appeared previously in the
following publications to which grateful acknowledgment is offered:
*Carolina Quarterly, Epos, Esquire, Impetus, New Southern Poets,
Poets of North Carolina, Southern Poetry Review,
The Girl in the Black Raincoat*

LIBRARY OF CONGRESS CATALOGING IN PUBLICATION DATA

Hardison, O   B
  Pro musica antiqua.
  I. Title.
PS3558.A6235P7   811'.5'4   77–3932
ISBN 0–8071–0295–4
ISBN 0–8071–0296–2 pbk.

Contents

*Pro
Musica
Antiqua*

Pro Musica
Antiqua

Listen to the music.
Listen to the sound of the krummhorn, the rebec,
The vielle, the virginal, the viola da gamba,
The scraping and twanging celebration of order.
It is all in the best possible order.
It streams up through the air of your house
And it is like summer,
A kind of sunlight slanting through the dust
Of almost empty air.

Throw away the dictionary.
Live where you are.
If the sackbut palls,
Bang on a pianoforte.
Limber up drums,
Unleash saxophones, let everything run wild.
Have voices, too, whole choruses of voices,
Doing the Nibelungenlied by ear.

This is the way it should be. Your house should be music.
Welcome it, hold on to it, sweat, let it pour into you
Like an old god making demigods with mortals.
Hold on until your every motion is dance.
Having received, enlarge.
When you let go, you will snore in C major.

I looked for you everywhere
Spent days in the happy forest of your hair
(What wilderness of trees, what shades with green commingled light;
I carved them all with anagrams of you),
Then moved to two bright lakes—your eyes—
Immersed, amazed, could breathe, finless,
My snorkel cast aside,
Floated, suspended in translucent tides;
Grown hungry, sought the pasture of your mouth
(Sweet mouth where sheep may safely graze),
To which, that it might thrive, I offered up
My quickening spirit.
Your neck, white minaret before which groveled on his dusty rug,
Sole traveler on that warm and throbbing desert,
This fedaheen of love.
And then—O then—and it was no mirage,
To glimpse two gentle hills.
To reach, after long journey, that warm and merciful snow
(If eyes give hope and kisses pledge fast faith,
How greater than these is charity);
To climb, after that holy pilgrimage,
Past freshets sprung from those tender slopes,
On mazy paths; to reach at last, the summits mastered,
Those rosy cupolas erected there,
By antique worshipers, to Cupidon.

As chance would have it, I had brought my book,
And pausing, opened. This the sacred text
And random oracle that struck,
As doves circled the blue and golden air,
Their voices chimes, my dazzled eye:
"Live, fairest Lesbia, let us live and love."

Chastised, I knew then: men seek glory on high mountain tops,
Yes, but neglect their love.
And knowing moved sadly on, but marked the spot,
Knowing I would return.
Descended, the sky filled with singing,
Found then my ship,
And sailed, for years it seemed, that creamy ocean.
"Turn back," the crew said (craven slaves),
"This is the edge, the edge, surely, of the world."
"Sail on," I said. At night,
Huddled on the afterdeck, the wake a phosphorus gleam
Floating under the moon, they plotted.
I watched my star, saw the heavens turn around it,
Knew my course, "Sail on," I said.

Those trades, as warm and gentle as a sigh,
Proved true; the currents, too, proved true;
So, when they spoke again, I nailed my heart,
A red medallion, to the mast: "Sail on."
Cowed, they worked the ropes.
And on that morning
When the sun from a coral sky first touched the sea
With shafts of splendor,
He on the mast, lashed to the perilous top
By my command, cried, "Land!"
And "Blessed land!" and after prayers
We named it Salvador.

In longboats, weeping, we broached its sloping sands,
Silent with wonder walked its fair meadows
(I thought: not more fair, fair Enna's garden
Where Proserpina, gathering flowers, by the dark god
Herself was gathered); past fragrant groves—
Cinnamon and thyme and mint—and there were flowers,

Wisteria, quince, flowering dogwood, trellis of rose, and without
    thorns those roses,
And others, more beautiful still, whose names I knew not.
Then on the rising slope,
A greater Hillary, I knew what it was to stand,
To stand at last, a god among men, at the center,
To feel creation roll around that place,
The stars and the planets too and the great sun and the moon,
All turning on that place.
I thought: till now I have seen through a glass darkly
But now stand face to face with truth. ‾
I planted my flag on that spot
(If time went by I did not know,
If space, it was annihilated)
And claimed it for my Empress.

I would have stayed, but now my crew,
Ungrateful rabble, babbled of home (what home could be but this?)
And kin and duty; and I, new geocentrist,
Owed still to scholars my discoveries.
By those pillars that support
Not walk but dance that swaying motion
Should be called,
More fair by far than those of Hercules,
For those the known but these the world's transcendent antipodes
Mark out, I then traversed.

Then carefully, all passion spent,
Returning, removed each pebble from the road,
For it is written: She must not dash her foot
Against a pebble;
And at my desk, at dusk,
I, Ptolemy, began to write this journal.

In the Palazzo
of Pellucid

Wherever he walked they talked in whispers
For his words were goblets of finest crystal
Each engraved with his initial, the famous crested P.
They were vessels of the wine of his meaning
Subtle vintages of red and white
Laid down from the good years of Pellucid.

His thought was a groaning table
Or rather many
To which Gaston LeNotre did service.
There was the pate of his Platonic triad
The caviar of his Nous
His wisdom a mean between the extremes of smoked salmon and
      melon balls
His love an omelet of agape
His shrewd intelligence and clear eye
(Heritage of peasant ancestors)
A bulwark to all, though touched with a splendid sadness,
Against the lawless speculation of chicken cacciatore,
The transcendent impulse, a vanity soon thwarted, of soufflé.
Simple elegance was his motto, impeccably served.

At noon he was pleased to walk in the gallery.
Spirits of the past dogged his footsteps.
Click, click, click his heels would go on the tiles.
Petitioned, would nod,
Surrounded by fire would talk candles to Dr. Ridley,
Connoisseur in the cathedral of Knowledge,
Keeper of its privy seal was Pellucid.

At night he would tune his violin
For they came at him from all sides,
Men with bold designs to circumvent ozone,
To stamp out the Pelagian heresy,
To publish his works in all languages;
Women desperately seeking love.

6

Hazang, hazang, hazang.
Sadness crouched by his bed.
Would shake himself, put on his smile,
Return to the restless masses
Strong in his white suit like the sun.
Entering, the babbling parliament grew silent.
Corrupt, and those the boldest, turned their glance aside.
The memory of pebbles rolled in his mouth,
The long sweep of the shore as he spread his robe,
His eyes piercing a thousand eyes.
"Cartago," he murmured; the roar of the sea replied;
Raising his arms, "Lacrimae," and pure streams of tears
          poured from their eyes;
"Genetrix" (for they loved him).
And ended demurely: "Ite, missa est."
He turned amid cries of assent
(Hands plucking his garment)
Thrust off the purple, walked home a citizen.

You, too, know Pellucid, passed by his house last night,
Heard the resplendent, agonizing cry of strings,
Moved forward, moved by that thought,
Into the shadow of his desolation.
Still he paces the floor, waiting,
Knowing duty and the tears of things:
Carthage to be destroyed, pieties served.
Also humble things:
The gods of threshold and of hearth
To be honored in a dark time.

Days he walks in the gallery.
Nights in another place, always playing.
Ignorant neighbors say, "Pellucid is playing.
He lives next door to Walter R. Clydesdale III."

What he failed to do is discriminate between art and art
        and art and art.
Everything he says is intelligible.
No foretaste of the drip, drip, drip.

It is not that the story ends badly,
Only that it lacks luster.
There should be an enchanting dawn—
The sky like wallpaper in a bordello—
A trellis of primroses;
Perhaps a rustling in the bushes.

Yes, and a central voice, too,
Because you need to get back from it, scrutinize it,
Stand on top of it and kick it
The way you would a stone.

Then there is that business about likeness and image.
That likeness is a seed
As sure as anything it will sprout pneumatic men.
(This could be full of significance for posterity.)
As for that image, an image is an image.
That is where art and art and art and art comes in.
Something you can hang up and pray to.
Sell to the tourists by thousands.
(It's a business like any other.)

But to get back, too much is left to the imagination.
A B C D E F G. There's verisimilitude for you.
Simple sensuous and passionate.
The whole story and everything connected.

Later on, that part on the Red Sea has color.
But two characters, a talking snake, and a *deus ex machina*.
And he pulls the plug just like that:
"The serpent beguiled me and I did eat."

After which everything goes drip, drip, drip.

Petition rejected.
Tell him to try painting.

The St. Petersburg Paradox

If you agree, agree to be indifferent.
The soul's exchange is strict: great speculators
May gain a world but mostly lose their shirts.

The talent that is death to hide is death
To risk upon the spinning of a wheel
And lose, and we are not elect and lose.

Luck is a dream. The odds are on the house.
Not lovers but accountants supervise
The black and crimson tables of the heart.

So kiss me and keep your love. Instead of light
We'll take the darkness and endure our passion
Nailed hand and foot to one another's fear.

Turn out the light, and then turn out the light.
We'll ease our pain, and when the day arrives,
Put on our emptiness and try to sleep.

Here in this room filled with leaving,
Sunlight on the bare floor,
A space almost empty,
You, most perfectly, are.
Earth, air, fire, and water be your elements,
And I your element.

I think how the bright sea extends its arms to the land
(The loving sea)
And falls back, and returns,
And falls back, and again, so you to me.

I, mariner, my boat obscure, explore
(But for one star lost, but that star fixed most truly at the center)
Most amazed, unmeasured you, through all those elements.

Earth: the dust that trembles at your touch.
Air: the dazzled air through which you move.
Fire: that turns the blood to smoking gold
(Most gentle fire). Water: it is your name.

Reach and touch me.
Leave, and return, and return, again and again.
Surround me, and in surrounding, as air in fire,
Be wholly light.

So shine that no darkness is.
All gold, and perfect be; be only splendor.
Never waver, for all know (for it must happen)
That all lights, even those most cherished,
Made of those mortal elements—
And for this most cherished are—are owed to darkness.

Colloquium
with Isis

To see the world as it is, said the professor,
Without the nonsense of perspective—
Tedious teleologies, the time machine,
Or Phyllis milking her nanny goat.

Wait, said Clockwatcher.
Would you deny the tick tock of things?
All those little cogs chewing away at each other?
Would you expect to get to here without now?

Beautiful, said Piet, wallpaper is beautiful.
Wallpaper doesn't lie. He said,
To the extent that you are yourself you are not wallpaper,
But you may realize yourself in wallpaper.

My point exactly, said the professor
(If there was a tock it was inaudible).
History—if I may be metaphoric—is a miracle.
It comes out of a bush.
It is given away free on mountains.
Somebody whispers it to a blind man.
Sometimes it is hatched out of an egg.

Somebody, he said, announces, this is ground zero.
Here I stand at the X, Y, Z of things.
Toward this place you have been marching and from here
        you will take your leave.
From this you will have natural pieties and archives.
For this you will draft armies,
And the ground will shake under their feet,
And rivers will drink the blood of their camels.

Ring. Piet. *Ring*. Clockwatcher. *Ring*. Everybody:
If I were you I would get down on my hands and knees in the dirt.
Look for your evidence in the scrabble, scrabble of archaeology.
Dismissed.

II
He was looking everywhere for the truth.
Did he really want it?
It is a product. We make it the way we make paper clips.
Not that truth is without its uses
Any more than the double negative
Of which there is no way with it, much less without it.

III
He was earning his way through to the answer.
Worked overtime, Sundays, holidays,
Waited tables, manned gas pumps, lifeguarded at swimming pools.
And he was honest and he knew patience.
Not for him your groping under the plackets.
Time enough for plackets after he had puzzled out the spoon,
Deciphered pliers, unraveled water.
No question, he deserved whatever he got.
He always slept on the floor with the window open.

What is it, Why?
People ask questions like that before, not after.
After, they have whatever answers there are.

Here is one:
You cannot leave this room without leaving it.
When you have gone you cannot come back.
You will see it in terms of next door.
There will be a different dandelion on the wallpaper.
When you look back, this room, which has all the shades half
      drawn,
Will be shaggy and golden.

If not, you would have no way of knowing.
Nobody gets anywhere without going.
If you are on a high wire: somersault.
If running from a freight train: dance.
If holding your own: wrestle it to the ground.

Next door is good because you will be in it.
In a sense, you are there already.
Even now, its dandelions sway to your shadows.
Soon everything will be obvious.

There will not be a single metaphor in all your sentences.
Whatever you say will be understood.
Already you know how it feels to be shaggy and golden,
And what it is to walk on a high wire and to run from a freight
      train and to hold on to what you are.
Risk everything now.
Next door you will meet . . . *one* . . . *two* . . . *three* . . .

Homage to
Alfred North Whitehead

You need to confront the obvious,
To stare it down,
To pursue the pickle to the utmost dill,
To see the world as green brine,
Creation as a peppercorn,
Brown, soft, puffy, drowning,
Distilling the sun, yes, and the stars and the moon too,
From the dill-colored firmament.
And then there are those large, green follicles
That bristle against the tongue.

As Dr. Whitehead said: "It takes an exceptional intelligence to
        contemplate the obvious."
I say: "Put your money where your mouth is."

Pythagoras knew the world is symbols.
Knew beans are evil.
Knew (as all lovers know) sheets after sleeping must be
    smoothed.
Measured the trembling of those strings
That tie the mind to the sky
In halfs and demi-halfs until it sings.

Never pick up what has fallen (pass it by).
Leave no mark on the ashes (you will not return).
Taste only bread that is shared.
And never, O never, look in a lighted mirror:
Those eyes will dazzle;
You will die in that radiant net if you come nearer.

The square of two arms on fire
Forms the hypotenuse of desire:
Become through others.
Never eat your heart (you were made for pleasure),
Or let swallows nest on your roof,
Or being infinite, accept a measure.

Middle
Passage

If Lazarus (says the great Pascal)
Dreams every night beneath the rain
He is the richest of them all,

While Dives surfeited in vain
Begs for a nightly crust of bread
Across the deserts of his brain,

Who is the loser; who's ahead?

Life is a toss—for every tail
You get a head with eyes to cry
And tongue to curse its last betrayal;

And every curse becomes a sigh
On lips grown passionate with tears,
And without words, there is no lie,
And if the cock crows, no one cares.

I staged the daffodils rather effectively, I thought.
I put them there just for you.
The crocuses came up a little vulgar—
A shade too blue, maybe—
And the grass so green it strained credulity.
It was the best I could do.

I put the sun on a string for you,
To hold it until it burst;
Bought you a bagful of stars.
I made the sky thunder and rain for you
When you were hurt,
And the waters shine where you washed your feet,
And the clouds were pillows under your head
Whenever you slept.

I wound up all the birds
And set them to go off under your window each morning
(I thought you should wake to music).

Wherever you walk, I put life.
Spirits dance in your breath.
Your voice is the sound of peace in that world.

Be my guest.
It's a nice little creation as these things go.

Umilissimo
to the Moon

O moon
Call me a root among flowers
Dark amid iridescence,
A swine among leopards, antelope, lambs
(Such sleek and fleet and soft as you admire),
A crow among swans.

But crow (and black as night)
My wings will lift me as no swan's
Up to your silver light,
Or swine, I can lurch through brambles,
Snorting, until I touch your sphere
Where it just touches the great circle of the earth,
Or root, a root endures,
Sends out more roots, is life,
Is gathered by moonlight,
Is moved inwardly by that light,
Is stirred to rise,
Powerful, sends its thick shoot upward
Until nothing at all can resist its motion
Toward you
O moon.

Prayer of
Umilissimo

Most high: all things are emblems of you.
Greet you when you rise, caress you before sleep.
At dawn the sky is huge with desire.
At noon each bush burns to embrace.
At night: At night the darkness whispers
Of good works accomplished in darkness.

Mysterious
Egg

Regard this quartz egg.
Transparent. Made in Mexico.
A fault runs slanting down its middle like a wall.

Philo Judaeus might have glossed it so:
This lesser egg expresses that greater egg
And that was hatched by the spirit that moved (the Hebrew here
Reads ejaculated) upon the waters.

That greater egg was round. Its shell laid out,
Came the albumen of the firmament,
The yolk of the sun (and light blossomed
Luxuriantly), and after, the stars and the moon,
So days grew separate from nights.
The sea filled up with water
Begetting all the creatures that swim there.
The land thrust out as from a watery womb
And from that land the creatures that lord it over the land
(Herbivores all then, for lions then grazed on hay)
And the insects, sucking and chewing, and all manner of worm.
Then great man,
And after, woman, to whom that great worm,
And after, man, on his belly, would crawl.
All that, Philo might say, came out of that greater egg.
When you see this lesser egg, think on these things.

Philogynists, poor worms crawling between heaven and earth,
Know better.
In the *Symposium* Aristophanes,
Then foolish fond to prey on fondest fools,
Told Socrates this story:

In the beginning everything was real.
Like all such things, each mortal was a sphere.
This made the gods angry, who said:
"Such spheres as these will reach beyond their sphere."
Like cordwood then they split those real men,
And since, each half
Has sought, disconsolate, its other half across that sphere
That is that greater egg.

This lesser egg, its fault translucently apparent,
Expresses me and me (that's you),
Each half one soul,
Or in each crystal half one lonely half,
Like day and night,
Together but separated by that fault.
Original sin,
A thought beyond gay Aristophanes,
Has made of perfect sphere this faulty egg.
                                        I kiss this egg.

I ask for some miracle to help those souls.
Let there be a passion hotter than yet imagined.
So hot that fault, grown soft
(Those two souls flowing softly together), will disappear.
So hot this adamantine egg,
Then pliable, will pull itself together,
And out of egg will grow again that sphere.

And yet, I knew no fault. That fault was yours.
You found it with some relics of the saints.
Until you gave it to me.
I was Columbus and my world was round.

I have become what I am.
There is now nothing in me that is not what I am.
All my roads lead to me.
I did not expect this to happen.

If I were an oak tree,
My leaves would be children,
Everything I love would be branches,
My enemies would be caterpillars,
My roots would be fastened deep in red clay.
You might then be, say, a bird. Something shining with
        impossible colors.
I would hold out my branches for you to roost in.
I would grow leaves to shade you.
I would give you my enemies to eat.
My roots would tremble with your singing.

If I were a building, I would have a baroque facade.
My windows would all be clean.
I would have a fountain—
Maybe *The Rape of Europa*—
And children would drink that water.
My walls would have mosaics, my floors *opus Alexandrinum*,
On my ceiling, the apotheosis of Marie Antoinette.
Your word for me would be house.

If I were the shore, every bay would have flags
To celebrate the powers of the sea.
My sand would be at your feet,
I would keep your seashells—
Tulips, razor clams, drills, olives, wentletraps—
For children on summer days.
At night your tide would cover me.
As we mingled, I would say:

Thank you, mother moon;
Thank you, father sun;
Thank you, thank you, thank you.

Every road meanders away from the center.
They all, in one way or another, go past your door.
Drive your triumphant car down any of them.
I will welcome you when you arrive.

The ABC
of Love

"Can we progress with ease from 'ox' to 'house'
to 'camel' to 'door' to 'lattice window' to 'nail'?" *

Can we progress? We can, remarked Pellucid, carelessly smiling.
Let us begin at the beginning:

Ox (the animal) rears its horns
Between which we, deliciously, are tossed.
Swart. Solid. Steaming through the nose.
Dragging his plow through the wounded earth,
Most heavy Alpha to most dear Omega.
There is some ease in this.
All farmers know it.

But more ease when, traces laid aside,
The farmer enters the house.
It is cool and swept, with a blue pottery jug of milk,
A loaf of bread with honey
Gold in the shadow, gift of B.

Easier now, but not easy, to C
What seems a needle's eye
To a camel, but may open easily
To him who stands patiently
Smiling through in pain: the door.
And moves forward as river flowing to Delta.

Know that mercy is easy. Is heavenly.
How even angels bow to human prayers.
Easily he enters, stirring with joys.
Closes the lattice window, nails it shut

*From a letter to the author. The words are the first six letters
of the Hebrew alphabet.

(Now day is only night)
With swift, ineFF-
Able nail.

Removes his overalls, holds in his hairy arms (and is held),
Surrounds (is surrounded by) his crop:
Earth, air, fire, water.
Holds everything, everything in his arms, is comforted, and
      murmers, "G."

What did you say your name was?

Lady, how was it when the gods sang?
For you were there. I know you, and you were there.
First music, then instruments,
Then radiant harmonies, plucked by intelligence from perfect
      frets.

For you the gods—the father of the gods himself—
Assumed old shapes:
Of earth, of flowing water, of coins sliding against your legs,
Of hills bloody with poppies where you walked,
Of mandrake crying from the battered earth.
The slavish salamander writhed at your feet,
The swan spread its wings for you,
The enormous bull that you with a thread controlled
Brought you to the source of dark rivers.

The Graces danced for you in sliding measures,
First Joy, then Grace, then Love with face averted.

When I touch you, reverent,
As one touched by the gods, I feel that music.
Tell me your name.

Odysseus
in Ithaca

The younger poets keep churning out propaganda:
"Beyond the Pillars of Hercules!" they write;
"On to Ultima Thule!"
Foundations come up with plans for expeditions.
I am always testifying before various committees.
Dedications enlist me in all kinds of worthy causes.

Here in my back yard
Under the olive tree
With nothing more than a pitcher of goat's milk
A slightly rancid piece of cheese
A little shade from the sun,
It feels good in spite of the flies.

The wars were good, of course.
I liked knowing what side I was on.
It is always a good feeling, too, to slit your enemy's throat,
To see the blood pour out of his mouth
(I never thought much of Hector
No matter what everybody said;
Suspected him of being a prig,
The invention of some propaganda machine, with that square
      chin,
Faithful wife, always well groomed, and all that;
Was glad when he was killed
If only because it ended a war that was becoming boring.

I looted Troy with the rest,
Impaled children on my pike;
Maddened in that glorious haze of blood and fire
Emptied myself time and time again
Into those terrified, cowed women;
Never looked back, never felt regret or had second thoughts)—
Everything was simple then.

If you draw a line, there is a right side and a left.
Put up a sun, there is day and night.
Pull out a map, you see east and west.
Nobody believed that drab soap opera about Helen and Menelaus,
But there was the matter of historical necessity,
The need to beat back the Asiatic hordes,
To keep the trade routes open,
Not to mention our essential freedoms.
So we took sides.
The lines then as straight as the edge of a sword.
I counted all the options: one, two, three, four.
Those lives and numbers, nothing escaped them, they held on to
      everything,
Held everything together.
Being products of the spirit, they were obeyed.

Only, somewhere on the road back, they lost their grip.
All those things, so unlikely, that happened,
They were beyond numbering.
All that suffering.
Who had ever seen a Cyclops,
Much less imagined that huge eye with a stake in it,
And that gigantic, hairy, improbable body racked with sobs,
Those stones he threw when he could not even see their target.

Who could anticipate Circe? (I enjoyed seeing them all turned to swine—
What they were, really, all along,
And reluctant, when I needed them for the ship, to be turned back.)
Those nights—who could anticipate them?
Adrift on that great pool bathed in light,
Gaining strength for the night.

Was it lust? Was it age?
The things of the spirit gradually became less important.
Numbers childish.
I gave up counting, threw away my ruler.
Ended the cult of personality.

Let Telemachus worry about the future.
He'll learn, as I did, there is nothing straight.
Everyone is maneuvering for power—
Bureaucrats, lobbyists,
Men with big ships and foreign connections.
Lust is impossible at my age.
Neither living nor dying offer anything especially interesting.

So here I am out in the back yard.
Penelope off to the dedication of the latest statue:
The Departure of Odysseus.
She's good at that, will say a few words, listen while the others talk.
Here in the back yard under the olive tree
There is a clod of dirt that defies intelligence,
Goat's milk I can hardly digest,
Cheese too hard to get my teeth into,
Those flies, as miraculous in their way as eagles.

Going buzz buzz buzz
One two three four flies
Buzz buzz buzz
Zigzagging around
Four three two one
Under the olive tree
Milk. Cheese the color of a burning city. Flies.

From the Metamorphoses
of Pellucid

Daphne

I cannot hear my voice.
A web of fine gold covers my eyes.
I have put on the full armor of the solar man.
More than constant, my shield blazes with your sign.
I enlarge, tumescent with light.

Daphne, possessed by the god, her long arms rising,
Helpless with love, moved, moves, changes.
Look through the leaves of her flesh:
Her veins are translucent, pierced everywhere by the sun.
Caressed, she opens, thrusts, sends up shoots;
Showering flowers on the ground,
Grows relentlessly skyward.

As shadow in this brilliance
Be rooted in earth.
Grapple it; draw strength from it to reach the sun.
Sway in its soundless music like the wind.
Love through these words: all my words are yours.

Flora

You know how it is.
One day you are walking naked through the desert.
You are a little flabby. It is cold and your feet hurt.
This boy comes floating out of the surrounding fog.
He begins whispering in your ear. His breath smells of crocuses.
You slim down. Sheerest georgette covers your body.
Even that is too much. You begin to sweat.
There is a warm wind blowing. Your hair begins to feel silky.
You feel like sitting down but the grass is full of changes.
You stumble over a daffodil, get tangled in periwinkle, stub your
    toes on dandelions.
Everything is turning green and yellow and blue.
You turn to say "thanks": your words come out buttercups and
    primroses.
Ahead of you three girls are dancing in a circle.
Their names are Euphrosyne, Aglaia, and Thalia.
They move smoothly through the shadow and sunlight.
There is no music. Where, at least, are the birds?
That man, who looks like a wrestler, is picking apples.
He is pointing upward through a break in the leaves.
He, too, is silent, waiting for something.
Don't let it worry you.
It will happen every year around this time.

Danaë

When I looked down she was like a coin in the water
But she blazed with her own glory.
The unreal is hard; but a god's philosophy is this:
If you want something, take it.
Being there among the stars
And the whole zodiac turning around me,
I felt her power.
Through Cancer, where its claws just touch the Milky Way,
Closing my ears with wax,
Drunk with the scent of honey, I descended.
Down I passed through the spheres
Their intelligences like sirens singing (but I could not hear)
Through fire, through air, to earth and blue water.

From the sky outside her prison, tell me, I shouted
(But she could not hear), what word will make you sigh,
What accent tremble, what touches burn if a god touches?
Her indifference was a furnace. It turned
My limbs to liquid gold. I flowed, diffused, became a mist,
And then I covered her: crept into every pore
And orifice; ran through the red mystery of her flesh like flame.
From my immortal essence she grew large.
I, drained and faint, slipped past that rosy net
And rose again to heaven through Capricorn.

Leda

Believe me: there is nothing up here as beautiful as flesh.
I watched it being made, pounded and beaten into shape,
That wild, cold earth breathed into until it breathed.
Invisible, saw it given a face to see,
Hair to shine, arms to open, hands to hold the rain and the sun;
Alone, a way to mark the road, tell east from west,
Drive a pole in at the center;
Dumb, a voice to call my name.

It was an outrage. I chained the one who did it to a rock,
Set birds at his liver and let him live.
For them (for stealing what was mine) I made sorrow
Which, when they found it, they called hope.

I made one a cloud and he made centaurs.
Gave him nothing and he poured hot life into it.
Hurled down, wrapped both arms around his scalding wheel
Halooing. One deformed brute, sparkling with pain,
Goes singing across my sky.

My image? I have no image. I will be anything—
Clown, hunter, bull, snow of gold, mere air—
Grovel before them in any shape they want.
Nothing I am (they know it)
Equals what they are.

This one sprawls, feeling her good weight, against a tree, an oak.
Looking down, my back prickles with down.
She makes it. Arms feathering, arching to cascades of feathers,
Down I float, singing soft gutturals.
She brushes her face with soft fingers,
Perspiring. O how I swell.
Neck, beak, bursting, eyes points on a single point.
And miracle for one with no pity
Am pitied. She folds me, is folded in these white wings.
For a god, to be even a beast is glorious.

I think of the sea changing and changing.
There is a long swell moving in from the Azores
Awash on the gray sand.
The sky unfolds into the water.
At Holden, Long Beach, Wilmington, Ocean Isle, Hatteras, Nags Head
The Outer Banks are ringing with explosions of light.
Clouds blossom in the water and the shore flames with the glory of their
        opening
As though God were making the world again.
Here I am, where the gentle sea touches the land,
And every name is new,
And every name is another name for the sea.

Stella
Maris

Star of the sea, surest point of brightness,
In the long darkness, compass point
For the poor traveler to whom, wild with longing,
Despairing of home, the skies for a moment open
(Mother of God, he says, let them not close)
To disclose that point, that quiet point
On which the nine spheres turn and their intelligence,
And sing, and rightly, only for you.
Stella Maris. Always bright. Always, never changing, yourself.

I want life to be a room.

A large room. Ordered. With books lining the walls.
Quiet. Where I can see myself leaning over a book
And there is sun in my hair and one other person
And the afternoon passes easily.

I want Mr. Stoudemire to be interested. Perhaps amused.
Nobody told me he would be nervous and shabby
And need breath freshener.
He would not be admitted to my country club.
He has stumbled and fallen and is broken.

Let the cup pass
Drink to the lass
Drink gin, drink whiskey, drink
Kirschwasser distilled from the blood of the Morello cherry.
In the big room that was my father's head I took a great scroll
And wrote with a man's pen:
Memo to personnel,
The Christmas card list, double-checking marital status and zip codes.
And later: A thank you note to Dr. and Mrs. Frankenstein.

It's cold in this room.
Do I have anything warm to put on?
If you look hard enough you can just make out how the light
Shimmers there on the dust, but then it moves.
Euclid alone has looked on beauty bare.
And Tom, Dick, and Harry.
It is hard keeping still.

There's something real,
Mr. Stoudemire. *There's* something real.
Put that in your pipe and smoke it.

This is the age of sentiment.
If it weren't for pain, I would not exist.
I feel, therefore I am.
Mr. Stoudemire, there is nothing you can do to budge me.

Listen to me.
Come out from behind your clippings and your opinions about the
        Secretary of Benign Amusements.
I want to get at you.
It was going to be quiet. Orderly. And you were going to tell me all
        the secrets.
And it would feel like being at the top of a high building
In a bright room with nothing cheap in it
And the light moving easily, all day, along the edge of the shadows.

I have visited temples, churches, shrines, tombs, and catacombs.
I have gone to all the right places at the best seasons.
Mr. Stoudemire, did you stay home?
Did you live? I mean, did you live?
Did you get drunk at the country club and sick at the
        Multiple Sclerosis Dance
And sleep with Tom, Dick, and Harry on the seven hills
And die under the stone pines of Battle Park?
I mean, did you get the stigmata?

Do you even care?
What do you really want, Mr. Stoudemire?
You never whispered anything to me.
You only said:
No Minotaur in this labyrinth
No god on this oak
No maypole in this piazza.
I also know: hog in sloth, fox in cunning, wolf in greed, sparrow in
        lust, and Tom, Dick, and Harry, and I can say all the dirty words.

The trouble with you, Mr. Stoudemire,
Is, I can see right through you. Right through you.
When you've got the stigmata, you're like that.

Hog in sloth, fox in cunning, wolf in greed, sparrow in lust.
We are in them but not of them.
Do you hear me, Mr. Stoudemire?
Do you hear me?
Here is what I am saying.
I am saying to hell with the annual meeting of the Association for
     the Advancement of Values.

Listen to that noise.
I hope this goddam thing isn't broken.

Madonna, be kind.
Arrange yourself so the light just strikes your face.
Reveal my fate.
I, instantly, slave though I am, am saved.
Now I can sing, and my canzon is this:
Amor vincit omnia.

God save me from geometry.
Let me be as simple as glass.

I have done with color.
Be absolute for white, your only color.
Imagine a central plain
Toronto to Winnipeg
Six feet in snow.
Covered. Except for a pine tree or two
Not a feature.
A blank from Winnipeg to Toronto.

How unique the sun!
A white fire
A cataract of glitter
Making the whole plain clatter with whiteness.
And there is also that wind
Whipping up a mist of snow,
And that mist is white
And through it the sun's rays
Strike again and again—

My God—and again and again—
Piercing and piercing
Until there is absolute white.

Almost absolute, anyway, because, remember, there is that tree.
And you can imagine what it is—
Some blue spruce or other
Heaving the snow from its green-blue spikes like a bottle fly
Shaking the dust from its back.
It has a shaggy bark
Crevassed and shadowed green-blue under branches dark as black.

If you look beyond to the whiteness,
To where all names run together,
If you think for a while down the milky path to paper white,
To eggshell, to bone, to natural, ultimate white,
Do you think, too, of Regina,
As drawn on an ivory sled by milk-white hinds
Across the snows of Saskatchewan to Manitoba,
To Manitoba where she shines with all the interior music of
       whiteness—
Crimson, green, gold, royal purple and the deepest blue—
With nothing of white or of black?

Small Talk
in a Garden

I will admit freely that it hurt.
In fact, it hurt like hell
Although I didn't notice it at the time.

Like a damn fool I fell asleep
(If I have any fault, it's being trusting)
And along comes the famous Doctor
Penknife in hand
And starts sawing away at my rib cage.
Some day they'll catch up to him.
Lift his license.
Sue him for every cent he's got.

Anyway, I woke up and there she was,
My first experience of society.
Going out where I go in,
Going in where I go out.
There was a reason for that, as I should have realized.

I suppose I was weak from loss of blood
Or still silly from the anesthetic
Or disoriented by shock.
Whatever it was, she got to me where I live.
Remember, we hadn't grown up together,
Gotten used to each other, to the differences, as you might say.

I suppose, too, I made all sorts of silly statements.
Probably a few promises that only a fool would keep
(Not that I realized it then—
Then everything looked rosy—
But it certainly did occur to me later
That I should have kept my mouth shut).

I wasn't after much
And, frankly, she didn't have all that much to offer.
I'd watched the animals go at it.
I knew the name for it even before I'd gotten through naming them.
When in Rome, I say, do as the Romans.

If she were honest (which she is not) she'd confess.
She liked it just as much as I did.
She only discovered later there was a hook in it.
The good Doctor again. This time he did it without a penknife.
Worked it so we betrayed ourselves,
Betrayed ourselves willingly, lovingly, enjoyed it even,
Jumped singing over the cliff.

So there we were rolling around in the grass
And might be there still, for all I know,
If she hadn't gotten hungry from all that exercise,
Gone foraging all over the blooming garden,
Brought back that fruit,
Held out on me until I agreed.
Hell, at that point I would have agreed to anything.

It was then I began noticing my side was hurting.
Ached when I got up in the morning,
And, believe me, ached when I got home at night after work.

Home, that's a laugh.
Home to the usual insipid boiled cabbage,
Jello with fake whipped cream
Laced with innumerable cancer-producing chemicals.
Home, to that deadly chit-chat about the boys
(Mostly Abel, a fairy if I ever saw one).

She's gone to fat now.
About as desirable as a water buffalo.
What with that and the pain in my side
I can hardly get it up any more.
None of that is as bad, however, as my uneasy feeling
That life may still hold one or two more surprises.

To a Late-blooming
Marigold

The last living thing in this garden is a marigold.
In the brown weeds around it I foresee
A spreading stain of mist and drizzle,
Reeds sheathed with ice,
Brown bundles on brown ribbons rolling to a gray-brown distance.

The greatness of a patch of brown grass
Is a splash of orange on a snowbank
Alive and smoking in the sullen air.
A vision as brown as coffee
Dripping through cracks in the ceiling of summer.

I see the death of a prince.
An old man shuffling, say, between A Street and the A & P
Was not found until morning.

So to this brazenly orange marigold
Drowning by the wall in brown weeds,
Brother, I say, it looks like a hard winter.
I'll sacrifice my heifer next March,
Smash it between the horns and slit its throat.
I only hope, brother, you know your part of the act.

Ambition is the young man's sinecure.
You know that life is motion to the last.
Your wealth will all go begging to the poor.
Your sailors will not cut you from the mast.

Beneath the lunar sphere all lines are straight
And you must turn and turn and turn again.
Catastrophes come knocking at the gate
And you must turn the key and let them in.

Your glassy girl is never what she seems.
Her body withers on the seamy bed.
Her floor is built on crooked enthymemes.
Her roof is turning over overhead.

God is a circle radiating birth.
You are refracted from the glistening flood.
Fertility is burning up the earth.
(I contemplate the Beautiful and Good.)

I said the dead have learned to cease to move.
Green conflagrations devastate the bride.
You are an ember in the emerald stove
And I, said Aristotle, and he cried.

Across the void's indifferent flood
The atoms drift like lazy snow;
In metaphysical cold blood
They'll kill the mind that thought them so.

Not warmth or light or subtle I
That's crucified on its own stick,
Or soundness or infirmity
Exist within the *Ding an sich*.

Outside titanic powers rave
And batter at our puny walls;
Let us be thankful for our cave
And whistle till the ceiling falls.

Yet I would gladly leave my home
For some remote and flowering south
And crush like honey from the comb
The naked sweetness of your mouth.

Umilissimo
at the Zoo

If feeding swans is what you want, feed swans.
Admire the articulation of their bones.
Bury your hand in 600,000 feathers.
Watch while they live; set your clock by their heedless snorts.
For their part, they will take what you give them.

Be careful; they are not your friends.
They are old, have looked the world in the face,
Have watched cities burn, heroes pour their lives into the mud.
Floating on black pools
They are wild, not emblems of peace.

Forget friendship.
Ask the old gods why you are here.
Do not feed swans: hunt them.
There are reasons for being you may have forgotten.

Malibu
with Rain

The race is always on the verge of tears.
Pull out the plug and watch the waters flow.
Twist any arm, insert your pinking shears,
Grab hold and pull on anyone's short hairs:
I guarantee the curling of the lip,
The quivering of the chin, the wrinkling brow,
The crumpling of the mask that is the face,
That are the signs infallible of tears.

"They also serve who only stand and wait."
It's also true the Devil lies in wait,
A barefoot clown with garlic on his breath.

I keep some few remembrances of death:
Memento mori, skeleton on strings,
My mother's skull, and several other things,
And I will leave them to you in the end.
Meanwhile, you cannot part me from my friend
Who pokes his dripping head into my head.
The sea is dying or already dead.
Everything is dying. Even the surf is still.
Wet, gray, cold, empty. Still.

Great O Antiphons
for Eastern Airlines

This lake of air is solid as a rock.
O cleave that rock and let the waters flow.
"Pull here" and exit in the undertow
To sink into the solid lake of air.
There fathom line has never touched the ground
And jangling symphonies delight the ear
That's tuned to hear the music of the air.

O curse that ear that never heard the sound
And kindred drum that never felt the shock
Of waters moving in the frozen rock
And spiral walls and chambers that inter
The springs and fountains of the lake of air.
*
No smoking please while we are on the ground.
This tar, this dust can quickly come to boil
So simmer gently, keeping your powder wet.

The heir of heir is not the air of soil.
It smokes and smokes and smokes without a sound.
O man of clay you'll bake in embers yet
Yourself will turn you terra-cotta brown,
Harder than shards of Ur or urns of Greece;
Your wings will wither . . .

                    Fasten seat belts please.
Farewell, my love, for you and I must part . . .
Harder than diamonds, harder than your heart.
*
O meat is bestial to your man of flight
Whose limbs are breezeways to the rustling wind.
Recall that for an apple Adam sinned.
By gluttony he fell and that was right.
So serve yourself instead upon this plate
Or pour yourself like quinine in this glass.

I thirst, I hunger, Lady, and I wait.
You must not let your effervescence pass.
Fly me:

For Lady, Love delights to found
His flimsy kingdoms miles above the ground.
His duchies, fiefs, and serfdoms have no need
For constitutions, legislatures, courts,
Prerogatives, or precedents, or torts.
Habeas corpus is your only right.
Your only rule *Attack*, sole duty *Breed*.
O marble pillars penetrate the light,
O sun press hotly esplanades and domes
Of Love's Madrids and Washingtons and Romes.

O air without end, O shuttle ride to bliss.
O never land. Why skyjack men from grace?

Dream
Prison

It is dark here. How can I wake?
Cold fires glaring through rivers of dark.
Blank openness, frozen; frozen hate.
Surprise to have come this way.

All sound is darkness and shuddering black,
Coiled like snakes sliding above the mind,
The mind recoiling and falling back.
No hope for an end.

The cold that blows here tortures all souls,
Brothers bought and sold. Bought and sold.
Crammed in the vaulting, shadows clutching the walls,
Cries like a flood from they crypt.

Cries and hands tearing blind faces.
No way to return. None. Ever.

Sharp
Flats

Rubble, dust, scum, marshes olive drab,
Lights like globes of fat floating on dishwater,
The light so gray you cannot see the wounds
The concrete pillars grind against the sky.
You've come into your own! Hail, Motherland!
Chaos of brickwork, ashes, cable drums,
Crushed cans, ash cans, soot, sooty canisters,
Uncanny reeds pointing like arrows. Dusty arrows.
I am tied to each pier, pillar, projection: pierce me.
Fire away, there are acres of me here.
You cannot miss this tarpaulin of skin.

No more! The saints can have Jerusalem,
Give me the pyramids and obelisks.
The Amtrack stops here on its way to Egypt.
Back through the Red Sea, craven Israelite.

Girl with Guitar

to S.G.

See those six high wires how her fingers
In a flickering dance (though random to my dazzled
Eye) defy the deep, and balancing on touch
Imponderable, measure the trembling lines,
Gamut from grumbling bass to glittering treble,
And strike the note of peril that we live.

And now involved in moving harmonies
Whose motions are the nations of the air
Whose time is pattern shifting in the light,
The heart grown reckless from those airs of grace
And tunes of glory, vibrates on its pegs,
And she, all glitter in the golden fields,
Alone and splendid, is its only song.

Reader of this poetry, stay.
I offer you undying fame,
And immortality of name,
But in return, you have to pay.

Virgil praised Caesar's feet of clay,
And Ovid praised his daughter's charm,
And Horace got his Sabine farm,
But rich Maecenas had to pay.

A mistress lives through Du Bellay,
While Spenser sang the Virgin Queen;
John Donne was witty but obscene,
But always, someone had to pay.

Rimbaud was just a little gay,
Maurice still more, Marcel the most,
But each knew how to tell the host
His duty to the Muse was—pay.

So rent me a house on Naples' bay
Where I can feel the tears of things
And think what song the siren sings
And how to make you, patron, pay.